THE COLONY

WRITTEN BY TOMMY DONBAVAND
ILLUSTRATED BY KEVIN HOPGOOD

Titles in Graphic Novels set

KANE STRYKER, CYBER AGENT
BY ROGER HURN & AMIT TAYAL

NIGHTMARE OF THE SCARECROWS
BY IAN MacDONALD & MARK PENMAN

THE HEAD IS DEAD!
BY TOMMY DONBAVAND & MARK PENMAN

THE COLONY
BY TOMMY DONBAVAND & KEVIN HOPGOOD

SPACE PIRATE UNICORN
BY DANNY PEARSON & PETER RICHARDSON

TERROR SWIPE
BY JONNY ZUCKER & PABLO GALLEGO

Badger Publishing Limited
Oldmedow Road,
Hardwick Industrial Estate,
King's Lynn PE30 4JJ

Telephone: **01438 791037**
www.badgerlearning.co.uk

2 4 6 8 10 9 7 5 3 1

The Colony
ISBN 978-1-78147-495-2

Text © Tommy Donbavand 2014
Complete work © Badger Publishing Limited 2014

Publisher: Susan Ross
Senior Editor: Danny Pearson
Illustration: Kevin Hopgood
Designer: Cathryn Gilbert

CONTENTS

Cast of Characters

Sam

Paul

Ellie

Vocabulary

absorb

acid

Commander

DNA

exoskeleton

experiment

grenade

soldiers

survive

technical

CHAPTER ONE

30th September. Almost a year to the day since the enemy first attacked, and Operation Abdicate is underway ...

Leading the team is Commander **Sam Thomson.**

Sergeant **Ellie Marks** is on technical duties.

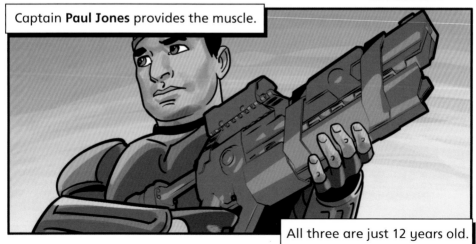

Captain **Paul Jones** provides the muscle.

All three are just 12 years old.

Bullets are useless against the enemy's hard exoskeletons, so the guns fire a sticky mixture of acid and ant DNA.

The ants absorb the mixture through valves called spiracles.

The acid melts the ant from the inside out.

Of course, that's not the only way to kill an ant ...

chapter three

So did you, but the mission ends here!

Paul! What are you doing?

Protecting my Queen!

GRAK!

Ants! They can smell DNA anywhere!

What the Queen can smell is the shared DNA between me and her first victim – my mum.

Take a closer sniff!

FzzzZZZZ!

The Queen can survive the acid pellet, but she will absorb my mum's hair. Now she smells of adult human, and you know what happens to them ...

The End

29

story facts

The inspiration for this book came from a 1954 black and white horror movie about giant ants called 'Them!'.

Giant or not – an ant can lift 20 times its own body weight. That's like a six-year-old picking up a car!

Ants don't have ears! They feel sound as vibrations though their feet.

Some species of ant live to be several years old, while others only have a lifespan of around 30 days.

The queen ant will lay thousands of eggs in her lifetime. Imagine trying to keep up with that many kids!

QUESTIONS

1. On what date did this final attack take place?

2. How old are Sam, Ellie and Paul?

3. What is mixed with ant DNA to make the deadly pellets?

4. What does Sam carry tied to his belt?

5. Which team member is wearing a mask?

Meet the Author

Tommy Donbavand spent his school days writing stories in which more popular kids than him were attacked and devoured by slavering monsters. Years later, he's still doing the same thing – only now people pay him for it. The fools!

Meet the Illustrator

Kevin Hopgood is a children's illustrator and comic book artist. He's worked on a wide variety of titles including 2000 AD, Games Workshop and Doctor Who. His most well-known work is on Iron Man for Marvel comics, where he co-created the character War Machine.